NOLCY
12/12

Rachel Carson

SPIRIT
of America®

RACHEL *Carson*

By Charnan Simon

Content Adviser: Linda Lear, Research Professor of Environmental History,
George Washington University, Bethesda, Maryland

The Child's World®
Chanhassen, Minnesota

6

RACHEL *Carson*

Published in the United States of America by The Child's World®
PO Box 326 • Chanhassen, MN 55317-0326 • 800-599-READ • www.childsworld.com

Acknowledgments
The Child's World®: Mary Berendes, Publishing Director

Editorial Directions, Inc.: E. Russell Primm, Editorial Director; Pam Rosenberg, Line Editor; Elizabeth K. Martin, Assistant Editor; Olivia Nellums, Editorial Assistant; Susan Hindman, Copy Editor; Susan Ashley, Halley Gatenby, Proofreaders; Jean Cotterell, Kevin Cunningham, Peter Garnham, Fact Checkers; Tim Griffin/IndexServ, Indexer; Dawn Friedman, Photo Researcher; Linda S. Koutris, Photo Selector

Photo
Cover: Stock Montage, Inc.; AP/Wide World Photos: 23, 26; Reprinted by permission of Frances Collin, Trustee, Copyright 2003 by Roger Allen Christie/Yale Collection of American Literature, Beinecke Rare Book and Manuscript Library: 6, 7, 8, 12; Reprinted by permission of Frances Collin, Trustee, Copyright 1941 by Rachel L. Carson/Yale Collection of American Literature, Beinecke Rare Book and Manuscript Library: 16; Photo by Mary Frye/Courtesy of the Lear/Carson Collection, Connecticut College: 9; Courtesy of the Lear/Carson Collection, Connecticut College: 14; Photo by Shirley Briggs/Courtesy of the Lear/Carson Collection, Connecticut College: 15; Photo by Rex Gary Schmidt/Courtesy of the Lear/Carson Collection, Connecticut College: 21; Photo by J. Lewis Scott/Courtesy of the Lear/Carson Collection, Connecticut College: 22; Bettmann/Corbis: 11, 13, 17; Alfred Eisenstaedt/Getty Images: 18, 25; The Ferdinand Hamburger Archives of The Johns Hopkins University: 10; Stock Montage, Inc.: 2.

Library of Congress Cataloging-in-Publication Data
Simon, Charnan.
  Rachel Carson : author and environmentalist / by Charnan Simon.
    p. cm. — (Our people)
"Spirit of America."
Summary: Provides a brief introduction to author and environmentalist Rachel Carson, her accomplishments, and her impact on American history.
Includes bibliographical references and index.
  ISBN 1-59296-011-1 (Library Bound : alk. paper)
1. Carson, Rachel, 1907–1964—Juvenile literature. 2. Environmentalists—United States—Biography—Juvenile literature. 3. Science writers—United States—Biography—Juvenile literature.
[1. Carson, Rachel, 1907–1964. 2. Biologists. 3. Environmentalists. 4. Scientists. 5. Women—Biography.]
I. Title. II. Series.
QH31.C33S46 2003
333.95'16092—dc21   2003004299

15   23   25

Contents

Chapter ONE	A Student of Nature	6
Chapter TWO	"Something to Write About"	12
Chapter THREE	Newfound Fame	18
Chapter FOUR	Silent Spring	24
	Time Line	29
	Glossary Terms	30
	For Further Information	31
	Index	32

A Student of Nature

Rachel Carson as a young girl

RACHEL CARSON WAS A SCIENTIST AND A WRITER who loved nature. She spent her life telling people about the beauty of the natural world—and warning them about the dangers of destroying that beauty. She was an early **environmentalist** whose work still helps protect our natural world today.

Rachel Louise Carson was born on May 27, 1907, in the little town of Springdale, Pennsylvania. While her older brother and sister were in school, Rachel and her mother happily roamed the countryside. Rachel loved being outdoors. She paid careful attention as her mother taught her to observe the

> The Little Brown House.
>
> Once upon a time, two little wrens were hunting a little house to set up housekeeping. All at once they saw a dear little brown house with a green roof. "Now that is just what we need," said Mr. Wreen to Jenny.

Rachel Carson began writing stories when she was a child.

world around her. Later, she would remember her childhood: "I was rather a solitary child, and spent a great deal of time in woods and beside streams, learning the birds and the insects and flowers."

When Rachel wasn't exploring nature, she could usually be found with her nose in a book. And if she wasn't reading, she was probably writing her own poems and stories. Rachel was just 11 when she had her first story published in the children's magazine, *St. Nicholas.*

Rachel's teachers weren't surprised. They knew that Rachel loved to write. She was an excellent student in all her classes and graduated as **valedictorian** of her high school class.

Interesting Fact

▶ Rachel Carson had five stories published in *St. Nicholas* magazine. She was paid $10 and made an "honor member" of the St. Nicholas League.

Her good grades earned her a **scholarship** to attend college.

Rachel arrived at Pennsylvania College for Women in nearby Pittsburgh in September 1925. In one of her first essays, she described herself as "a girl of eighteen years, a Presbyterian, Scotch-Irish by ancestry, and a graduate of a small, but first class high school." Then she listed all the things she liked, ending with "I love all the beautiful things of nature, and the wild creatures are my friends."

Rachel thought she would study English literature in college. Her dream was to become a professional writer. But when she took a **biology** class with a teacher named Mary Scott Skinker, her dream changed. Rachel was inspired by Miss Skinker's love of science. It reminded her

Rachel Carson (right) and Pennsylvania College for Women English professor, Grace Croff

of her own love of nature. Rachel decided to become a scientist, too.

This was a daring decision for Rachel. In the 1920s, there weren't many female scientists. Some people thought women weren't smart enough to be scientists. Rachel knew she would face many obstacles. She knew she might have a hard time earning a living. But she didn't care. She was determined to make her dream of being a scientist come true.

Miss Skinker was proud of Rachel. She helped her get a scholarship to study at the famous Marine Biological Laboratory at Woods Hole, Massachusetts, for a summer. Rachel loved her time at Woods Hole. Ever since she had been a child, she had loved reading about the ocean. She longed to see the wild waves and quiet tidepools for herself. Finally, at

Rachel Carson spent a summer studying at the Marine Biological Laboratory at Woods Hole, Massachusetts.

Interesting Fact

▶ While she was in college, Rachel Carson wrote for the student newspaper, *The Arrow,* and the literary magazine, *The Englicode.* She also helped start a science club called Mu Sigma Sigma.

THE JOHNS HOPKINS UNIVERSITY
BALTIMORE

APPLICATION FOR ADMISSION TO THE FACULTY OF PHILOSOPHY

I. Date.   April 27, 1928

II. Name (*in full*), year and place of birth, and home residence.
    Rachel Louise Carson
    Date of birth May 27, 1907, in Springdale, Pennsylvania
    Home residence 534 Colfax Lane, Springdale, Pennsylvania

III. Name of parent (or other relative) and his post office address.

    Robert W. Carson
    534 Colfax Lane
    Springdale, Pennsylvania

IV. (*a*)* Name the institutions in which you have studied, the time of your residence in each,
    and the degrees which you have received, if any, with dates.
    Pennsylvania College for Women, Pittsburgh, Pennsylvania
    Three years, beginning September, 1925

    (*b*) Time spent otherwise, with dates, since entering college (including foreign travel.)

V. Name the subjects that you plan to pursue. Zoology, with special emphasis on
Genetics and Comparative Anatomy. Specific courses as follows:
Genetics and Development, General Physiology of Animals, Vertebrate
Zoology, Investigations, German, English Literature, Vertebrate Embry-
ology, and Physics and Chemistry as recommended by the Director of
VI. Do you expect to apply for a higher degree? the Department.

    I expect to apply for the degree of Master of Arts in 1930.

VII. I recognize the right of the University to exclude at any time a student whose conduct or aca-
    demic standing renders his or her presence undesirable in the institution.

                                R. W. Carson
                    Signature of Applicant, if of age; otherwise, Parent or Guardian.

* This application blank must be accompanied by a transcript of your college work (and university work, if any),
unless you have pursued all of your courses in this University.

In 1928, Carson applied for admission to graduate school at Johns Hopkins University.

Woods Hole, she could do all that. It was one of the happiest summers of her life.

Miss Skinker also helped Rachel get into graduate school at Johns Hopkins University in Baltimore, Maryland. Rachel studied hard at Johns Hopkins. She earned her **master's degree** in **zoology** in 1932. She wanted to keep studying and earn her **doctorate.** But even with scholarships and what she earned by teaching part-time, she simply did not have enough money to continue her studies. By 1934, Rachel had to leave school and start working.

10

WOODS HOLE, MASSACHUSETTS, IS A LOVELY SEASIDE VILLAGE ON CAPE COD. It is also one of the best places in the world to study oceanography—the science that deals with the oceans and everything in them. Scientists and teachers have been using Woods Hole as an educational center since 1871.

When Rachel Carson studied there in the summer of 1929, the center was known as the Marine Biology Laboratory at Woods Hole. Today, it is called Woods Hole Oceanographic Institute. Woods Hole has laboratories onshore for scientists to do research in. It has boats to take people out to sea, for exploring the ocean up close. It even has a small, deep-diving submarine for studying life in the ocean depths. Woods Hole is a wonderful place for scientists to work together to learn about the mysteries of the sea.

Chapter Two

"Something to Write About"

After she left graduate school, Rachel lived with her parents, Robert and Maria Carson.

IN 1934, THE UNITED STATES WAS IN THE middle of the Great Depression. Millions of people were out of work. It was not a good time to be a young female biologist just starting her professional life.

Rachel was living in a rented house in Baltimore with her parents. She and her mother were still very close. They had missed each other terribly when Rachel went to graduate school. They were glad to be together again. The Carson household also included Rachel's sister, Marian, and Marian's two daughters. Marian was ten years older than Rachel and was divorced. Now she was ill with **diabetes** and needed help caring for young Virginia and Marjorie.

Times were hard. Rachel felt lucky to find part-time teaching jobs. Mr. Carson and Marian worked when they could, while Mrs. Carson cooked, kept house, and helped watch the young girls. Then, in July 1935, Rachel's father died of a heart attack. Now, more than ever, it was up to Rachel to support her family.

Hundreds of people waiting in line to apply for jobs during the Great Depression.

Again, Miss Skinker helped. She coached Rachel for the **civil service** exam, which would help her get a job as a government scientist. Then she urged Rachel to call on a man named Elmer Higgins in Washington, D.C.

Higgins worked for the U.S. Bureau of Fisheries. When Rachel visited him, he was desperate. He needed someone to write a series of radio broadcasts about life under the sea. Professional authors didn't know enough about oceanography. Professional scientists didn't know enough about writing good stories.

It was a perfect job for Rachel Carson. She wrote one sample "fish tale" and was

Interesting Fact

▶ Even with scholarships, Rachel Carson's family had a hard time putting her through college. Rachel's mother gave piano lessons and sold chickens, apples, and even the family china to pay for college expenses. Rachel tutored high school students in the summer to earn extra money.

A portrait of Rachel Carson taken during the time she worked for the U.S. Fish and Wildlife Service

immediately hired to write the rest. It was only part-time work, but for the first time, she was combining her two loves—writing and science—to earn a living. Years later, Rachel remembered how exciting this was: "I thought I had to be one or the other. It never occurred to me—or apparently to anyone else—that I could combine the two careers. It dawned on me that by becoming a biologist, I had given myself something to write about."

Within a year, Rachel was working full-time for the Bureau of Fisheries. Her official title was junior **aquatic** biologist, but she did more writing and editing than research.

Rachel and her mother moved to Silver Spring, Maryland, to be closer to her job. Things were looking up—and then Marian died. Virginia and Marjorie came to live with Rachel. Now she was responsible for supporting a family of four.

It was a busy time. Carson worked hard for the bureau. She wrote and edited articles and answered questions people sent to the bureau. She paid attention to the research other scientists were doing. At night, she used what she was learning to write articles for the local newspaper. In her spare time, she took Virginia and Marjorie on nature hikes, just as her mother had done when she was a child.

In 1937, Carson wrote a longer essay, titled "The World of Water." This article captured beautifully what life was like for sea creatures at home in the ocean. She was thrilled when her essay was printed in a famous national magazine called *The Atlantic Monthly.* She was even more thrilled when a New York publishing house asked her to expand her essay into a full-length book.

Rachel Carson loved being outdoors and went on nature hikes whenever she could.

Carson worked on her book for more than two years. She did field research whenever she could. She spent a lot of time in libraries. She read, researched, and read some more. She still had her job at the Bureau of Fisheries, of course, so she could only write late at night and on weekends. When *Under the Sea-Wind* was finally published on November 1, 1941, **reviewers** praised it highly.

Now the sun dipped deeper below the horizon; the greyness of the nights deepened; the hours of twilight lengthened. ~~Now~~ the rains that came more often and lashed with sharper violence were matched by a gentler rain as the flowers of the tundra dropped their petals. ~~in token of the passing of another summer.~~ The foodstuffs - the starches and the fats - had been stored away in the seeds to nourish the precious embryos, into which had passed the immortal substance of the parent plants. The summer's work was done. No more need of bright petals to lure the pollen-carrying bees; so cast them off. No more need of leaves spread to catch the sunshine and harness it to chlorophyll and air and water. Let the green pigments fade. Put on the reds and yellows, then let the leaves fall, too, and the stocks wither away. Summer is dying.

Soon the first white hairs appeared in the coats of the weasels, and the hair of the caribou began to lengthen. ———>

Interesting Fact

▶ *Under the Sea-Wind* focused on three different types of creatures—seabirds, mackerels, and eels. Although she named some of her animals, the real main character of the book was the ocean itself. In clear, lovely language, Carson told what life in the ocean was like.

Unfortunately, the book didn't sell well. Just one month later, on December 7, 1941, the Japanese attacked the U.S. navy base at Pearl Harbor in Hawaii. Suddenly, the United States was at war. People were more interested in reading newspaper articles about the fighting than in reading a book about the beauties of ocean life. This was a disappointment for Carson.

RACHEL CARSON LIVED THROUGH TWO OF THE MOST TERRIBLE EVENTS IN modern history. She attended graduate school and was just starting work during the Great Depression. The Great Depression was a worldwide business slump that began in 1929 and lasted throughout most of the 1930s. During the Great Depression, millions of people around the world lost their jobs, their homes, and their savings. Banks ran out of money. Stores and factories closed down. Some countries even changed their leaders and types of government to try to battle the hard times. In the United States, the Great Depression didn't really end until 1942, after the country entered World War II.

World War II was fought from 1939 until 1945. More than 17 million soldiers from all over the world were killed. Many more ordinary people—men, women, and children—also died. World War II began on September 1, 1939, when Germany invaded Poland. Soon the fighting spread throughout Europe, Africa, and Asia. The United States didn't enter the war until Japan attacked the U.S. naval base at Pearl Harbor in Hawaii on December 7, 1941. World War II ended after Germany surrendered on May 7, 1945, and Japan surrendered on September 2, 1945.

Chapter THREE

Newfound Fame

THE WAR YEARS WERE HECTIC FOR RACHEL Carson and her coworkers. Their offices were moved from Washington, D.C., to Chicago, Illinois—and then back again. Carson was promoted to assistant aquatic biologist, then to associate aquatic biologist, and finally to aquatic biologist. She helped put together information on ocean currents and depths, to help the army and navy. She wrote a series of pamphlets about the advantages of eating fish, so meat could be saved for soldiers fighting overseas. She even managed to write a few articles of her own. And whenever she had a spare minute, she went on early morning bird-watching walks and

Carson (front and center) enjoyed going on bird-watching walks during her free time.

nature hikes with her mother, her nieces, and her friends.

By 1949, Carson had been promoted to editor-in-chief of publications for the U.S. Fish and Wildlife Service (the new name for the Bureau of Fisheries). It was like being in charge of a small publishing house. Carson and her assistants worked with authors, illustrators, designers, and printers. Together, they published every bit of printed material that came out of the government office.

One project that Carson especially enjoyed was a series of booklets called *Conservation in Action.* She traveled to wildlife refuges and nature reserves around the country, doing research. She wanted all Americans to understand how important it was to protect the places where wild creatures lived.

Even this series wasn't enough to satisfy her. Carson wanted to write another book about the ocean. As she told an oceographer friend, "I am much impressed by man's dependence upon the ocean, directly, and in thousands of ways unsuspected by most people. These relationships, and my belief that we will become even more dependent

▶ Rachel Carson said that *Under the Sea-Wind* was her favorite book. She dedicated the book to her mother, in thanks for her lifelong love and support. As for her writing style, Carson said, "Given the initial talent … writing is largely a matter of application and hard work, of writing and rewriting endlessly until you are satisfied that you have said what you want to say as clearly and simply as possible…. If you write what you yourself sincerely think and feel and are interested in, the chances are very high that you will interest other people as well."

upon the ocean as we destroy the land, are really the theme of this book."

Carson worked on her book for several years. She went deep-sea diving in the Florida Everglades and spent 10 days on a research ship in the North Atlantic. She scoured libraries for books, articles, and journals. She wrote to and visited scientists and oceanographers around the world. She wanted her book to be perfect.

When *The Sea Around Us* was published in 1951, it became an instant best-seller. Readers were fascinated by Rachel's view of the **ecology** of the ocean. They loved the way she described undersea plants and animals. They were impressed at how easily she explained the complex science of tides, currents, and waves in clear, yet poetic, language.

Suddenly, Rachel Carson was famous. People wanted to interview her on radio and television. She was invited to give speeches and sign autographs. Newspapers and magazines wanted to take her picture.

Carson was glad people liked her book. She was happy to share her love for the ocean. She was even happier because the book's success meant she could leave her job at the Fish and Wildlife Service and spend all her time writing. Carson could hardly wait to get back to Woods Hole to begin re-searching her next project. Now she wanted to write a book about ocean coastlines that would "…take the seashore out of the category of scenery and make it come alive." When *The Edge of the Sea* came out in 1955, it, too, was an instant best-seller.

Carson and illustrator Bob Hines working on Key West

Finally, Carson was writing the kinds of books she'd always dreamed of. But she was impatient with people who seemed surprised that books about science could be popular. She didn't see science as separate from life or from literature. She spoke out on this in a speech:

> This notion that "science" is something that belongs in a separate compartment of its own, apart from everyday life, is one that I should like to challenge…. The materials of science are the materials of life. Science is part of the reality of living;

it is the what, the how, and the why of everything in our experience. It is impossible to understand man without understanding his environment…. The aim of science is to discover and illuminate truth. And that, I take it, is the aim of literature…. It seems to me, then that there can be no separate literature of science.

For the first time in her life, Rachel had enough money to build a small cottage on the Maine coast, where she and her mother spent every summer. She built another house in Silver Spring, Maryland, where they lived in winter.

But not everything was easy. Rachel's nieces, Virginia and Marjorie, had grown up by now. Virginia was happily married and lived nearby. But Marjorie was often ill. She had a young son, Roger, whose father was not involved in their lives. Then, in 1956, Marjorie died. Rachel adopted five-year-old Roger. Now she had another child to raise.

Rachel Carson with her grandnephew Roger and her friend Ruth Scott

IT'S HARD TO IMAGINE THE excitement that *The Sea Around Us* caused. Before it was published in book form, a shortened version was printed in the notable literary magazine, *The New Yorker.* Later, it was condensed in *Reader's Digest,* another famous magazine. The book became a Book-of-the-Month Club alternate selection, which guaranteed that thousands of people would read it. It won the National Book Award (above) for nonfiction and the Burroughs Medal for outstanding nature writing. The *New York Times* voted it the out-standing book of 1951. *The Sea Around Us* stayed on the best-seller lists for almost two years and was eventually translated into 32 languages. It was even made into a movie. Although Rachel Carson didn't think the movie was very true to her book, it won an Academy Award for Best Documentary.

Carson herself was honored by the Geographical Society of Philadelphia, the New York Zoological Society, the Royal Society of Literature in England, Theta Sigma Phi (the national fraternity of women in journalism) and even the Department of the Interior. Several colleges and universities awarded her honorary degrees.

Because *The Sea Around Us* was so popular, Rachel's publishers decided to reissue her first book, *Under the Sea-Wind.* It, too, became a best-seller and was named a Book-of-the-Month Club alternate. Carson was uncomfortable with all the demands made by her newfound fame. But she was delighted that her writing was finally receiving the recognition it deserved.

Silent Spring

▶ *Silent Spring* appeared in the *New Yorker* magazine before it was published in book form. It became a Book-of-the-Month Club selection and stayed at the top of the *New York Times* best-seller list for more than six months. More than 500,000 copies of the book were sold. And between 10 million and 15 million people learned about the book when they watched the *CBS Reports* television show titled "The Silent Spring of Rachel Carson."

IN JANUARY 1958, RACHEL CARSON GOT A letter from her friend Olga Owens Huckins. Her friend's neighborhood had been sprayed with **pesticides** to kill mosquitoes. Huckins was concerned because songbirds and nesting robins were also dying. Wasn't there anything Carson could do?

Carson had been concerned for many years about the dangers pesticides presented to the natural world. Modern science had produced many new chemicals. Some were used to kill insects that damaged crops and spread disease. The chemical companies said these pesticides were safe. The federal government supported the chemical companies. But Carson knew that many of her scientist friends were worried. They didn't know how the chemicals might hurt animals, people, or the environment.

Carson decided to find out just how dangerous pesticides were. She spent five years quietly doing research. She read everything she could about how pesticides were used—and misused. She talked to experts and wrote letters to scientists all over the world. She checked and double-checked every single fact. There was so much to learn that she had to hire research assistants to help her.

Carson working at home with her microscope

The more Carson learned about pesticides, especially a chemical called DDT, the more horrified she became. DDT was everywhere—on the apples children packed in school lunches, on crops like corn and wheat and soybeans, and in the feed that cows and pigs and sheep ate. DDT was in rivers and oceans and lakes. It was part of the whole **ecosystem**—and it was dangerous. DDT made people and animals sick. It made birds' eggshells so thin, they broke before the baby birds could hatch. As far as Carson was concerned, DDT was a poison. It should never have been used without warning people how dangerous it was.

Carson spoke about the dangers of pesticides at government hearings in Washington, D.C.

Carson put all she had learned into a book called *Silent Spring.* The title was a reminder of what our world would be like without the beauty of the spring birdsong. But the reaction to her book was anything but silent. Reviewers called the book "shocking and frightening." Readers furiously demanded to know why they had never been warned about the dangers of pesticides. Chemical companies just as furiously denied that their products might be harmful.

The uproar spread into the federal government. President John F. Kennedy created a special committee of scientists to study pesticides. This committee agreed with Carson's conclusions. Pesticides were much too dangerous to use without stricter controls and more research.

Eventually, DDT was banned in the United States. Over time, other pesticides have been banned as well. Congress began passing laws to protect the environment from pesticides and other kinds of pollution. Later, a government agency called the Environmental Protection

Agency was formed to help even more. The Clean Air and Clean Water Acts followed soon after.

Carson didn't believe that one book could change the world. But some people did. As one senator told her, "Miss Carson, every once in a while in the history of mankind, a book has appeared which has substantially altered the course of history. Your book is of that important character, and I feel you have rendered a tremendous service."

Carson was pleased. As she wrote to a friend, "The beauty of the living world I was trying to save has always been uppermost in my mind—that, and anger at the senseless, brutish things that were being done. I have felt bound by a solemn obligation to do what I could—if I didn't at least try, I could never again be happy in nature."

Only her closest friends knew that Carson didn't have much time left. Even as she was writing *Silent Spring,* she was dying of cancer. *Silent Spring* was published in 1962. For the next two years, Carson struggled through illness and the uproar surrounding her book. Then, just before sunset on April 14, 1964,

Rachel Carson died. She was only 56 years old.

Carson died too young, but her legacy lives on. Through her books, she has taught people to look at nature with new eyes. She reminds us that humans aren't separate from the natural world, but a part of it—and that we have tremendous power to help or to harm Earth's ecosystems.

Carson is often called the founder of the environmental movement, for her fight to save the natural world. But the battle isn't finished. DDT has been banned in the United States, but it is still used in other parts of the world. New chemicals—some just as dangerous as DDT—are still being used in our own country. Water, air, and soil pollution still exist. Plants, animals, and humans are still at risk.

Rachel Carson's greatest joy was to learn about and honor our natural world. As she said, "The pleasures, the values of contact with the natural world are not reserved for the scientists. They are available to anyone who will place himself under the influence of a lonely mountain top—or the sea—or the stillness of a forest; or who will stop to think about so small a thing as the mystery of a growing seed."

1907   Rachel Louise Carson is born on May 27 in Springdale, Pennsylvania.

1917   Carson has her first story published in *St. Nicholas* magazine.

1925   Carson goes to Pennsylvania College for Women in Pittsburgh.

1929   Carson graduates from college and spends the summer studying in Woods Hole, Massachusetts.

1932   Carson earns her master's degree in zoology from Johns Hopkins University in Baltimore, Maryland.

1934   Lack of funds forces Carson to leave Johns Hopkins without completing her doctorate degree.

1935   Carson's father dies. She begins writing radio scripts on undersea life for the U.S. Bureau of Fisheries.

1936   Carson is hired as a full-time junior aquatic biologist with the Bureau of Fisheries. Her sister, Marian, dies. Her nieces, Virginia and Marjorie, come to live with Carson and her mother.

1937   The *Atlantic Monthly* publishes Carson's article, "Worlds of Water."

1941   Carson publishes her first book, *Under the Sea-Wind.* The United States enters World War II.

1949   Carson becomes editor-in-chief of all U.S. Fish and Wildlife Service publications.

1951   *The Sea Around Us* is published and wins the National Book Award and the Burroughs Medal for excellence in nature writing.

1952   *Under the Sea-Wind* is re-released and joins *The Sea Around Us* on the bestseller list. Carson leaves the Fish and Wildlife Service to become a full-time writer.

1955   *The Edge of the Sea* is published and becomes a best-seller.

1956   Carson adopts her five-year-old grandnephew after her niece Marjorie dies.

1958   Carson's mother dies.

1962   *Silent Spring* is published to worldwide acclaim.

1963   President John F. Kennedy's Science Advisory Committee endorses Carson's views on using pesticides.

1964   Carson dies of cancer on April 14 in Silver Spring, Maryland.

1965   *The Sense of Wonder* is published.

Glossary Terms

aquatic (uh-KWOT-ik)
Aquatic means having to do with water. An aquatic biologist is a scientist who studies things that grow or live in water. Rachel Carson was promoted to aquatic biologist for the U.S. Bureau of Fisheries.

biology (bye-OL-uh-jee)
Biology is the scientific study of living things. Rachel Carson studied aquatic biology.

civil service (SIV-il SUR-viss)
Civil service refers to work done for government departments. Miss Skinker helped Rachel Carson study for the civil service exam.

diabetes (dye-uh-BEE-teez)
Diabetes is a serious disease in which the body does not produce enough of a hormone called insulin. Rachel Carson's sister suffered from diabetes.

doctorate (DOK-tuh-ruht)
A doctorate is the highest degree given by a college or university. Rachel Carson didn't have enough money to stay in school to complete a doctorate degree in zoology.

ecology (ee-KOL-uh-jee)
Ecology is the branch of biology that studies living things in relation to their environment and to one another. *The Sea Around Us* described Rachel Carson's view of the ecology of the ocean.

ecosystem (EE-koh-siss-tuhm)
An ecosystem is a network of relationships among living things and their environment. Pesticides can do great harm to Earth's ecosystems.

environmentalist (en-vye-ruhn-MEN-tul-est)
An environmentalist is a person who works to preserve and protect our natural environment. Rachel Carson was an early environmentalist.

master's degree (MASS-turs di-GREE)
A master's degree is given by colleges and universities to students who have completed studies beyond the basic college degree. Rachel Carson earned a master's degree in zoology.

pesticides (PESS-tuh-sides)
Pesticides are chemicals used to kill insects or other pests. *Silent Spring* alerted people to the dangers of pesticides.

reviewers (ri-VYOO-ers)
Reviewers are people who give their opinions about books, plays, movies, etc. *Under the Sea-Wind* was highly praised by reviewers.

scholarship (SKOL-ur-ship)
A scholarship is a grant of money or other kind of aid that helps a student continue his or her studies. Rachel Carson was awarded a scholarship for college.

valedictorian (val-uh-dik-TOR-ee-uhn)
A valedictorian is the student who graduates with the highest academic ranking in the class. Rachel Carson was the valedictorian of her high school graduating class.

zoology (zoh-OL-uh-jee)
Zoology is the science that deals with the study of animals and animal life. Rachel Carson studied zoology throughout her life.

For Further INFORMATION

Web Sites

Visit our homepage for lots of links about Rachel Carson:
http://www.childsworld.com/links.html

Note to Parents, Teachers, and Librarians:
We routinely verify our Web links to make sure they're safe,
active sites—so encourage your readers to check them out!

Books

Archer, Jules. *To Save the Earth: The American Environmental Movement.* New York: Viking, 1998.

Carson, Rachel. *The Sense of Wonder.* New York: Harper & Row, 1965.

Goldberg, Jake. *Rachel Carson: Biologist and Author.* New York: Chelsea House Publishers, 1992.

Stewart, Melissa. *Rachel Carson: Biologist and Writer.* Chicago: Ferguson Publishing Company, 2001.

Places to Visit or Contact

Rachel Carson Homestead Association
To write for more information about the birthplace and childhood home of Rachel Carson
P.O. Box 46
Springdale, PA 15144
724/274-5459

Rachel Carson National Wildlife Refuge
To visit a wildlife refuge named for Rachel Carson and learn more about the importance of these lands to migrating waterfowl
321 Port Road
Wells, ME 04090

Index

The Atlantic Monthly (magazine), 15

Baltimore, Maryland, 10, 12
Book-of-the-Month Club, 23, 24
Burroughs Medal, 23

Carson, Maria (mother), 12, 12, 13, 22
Carson, Marian (sister), 12, 13, 14
Carson, Rachel, 6, 8, 9, 12, 14, 15, 18, 21, 22, 25, 26
    birth of, 6
    childhood of, 6–7, 7
    death of, 28
    education of, 7–10, 10, 13
    health of, 27
Carson, Robert (father), 12, 12, 13
Carson, Roger (grandnephew), 22, 22
Clean Air Act, 27
Clean Water Act, 27
Conservation in Action (booklet series), 19

DDT (pesticide), 25, 26, 28
Department of the Interior, 23

The Edge of the Sea (book), 21
Environmental Protection Agency, 26–27

Geographical Society of Philadelphia, 23
Great Depression, 12, 13, 17

Huckins, Olga Owens, 24

Johns Hopkins University, 10

Kennedy, John F., 26

Marine Biological Laboratory at Woods Hole, 9–10, 11, 11

Marjorie (niece), 12, 14, 15, 22

National Book Award, 23
New York Times (newspaper), 23, 24
New York Zoological Society, 23
The New Yorker (magazine), 23, 24

oceanography, 11, 13–14

Pearl Harbor, Hawaii, 16, 17
Pennsylvania College for Women, 8
pesticides, 24–25, 26–27, 28
Pittsburgh, Pennsylvania, 8

Reader's Digest (magazine), 23
Royal Society of Literature, 23

The Sea Around Us (film), 23
The Sea Around Us (book), 20–21, 23
Silent Spring (book), 24, 26
"The Silent Spring of Rachel Carson" (television show), 24
Silver Spring, Maryland, 14, 22
Skinker, Mary Scott, 8, 9, 10, 13
Springdale, Pennsylvania, 6

Theta Sigma Phi fraternity, 23

U.S. Fish and Wildlife Service, 14, 18, 19
Under the Sea-Wind (book), 15–16, 20, 23

Virginia (niece), 12, 14, 15, 22

Woods Hole, Massachusetts, 9, 11, 21
Woods Hole Oceanographic Institute, 11
"The World of Water" (essay), 15
World War II, 17, 17

About the Author

CHARNAN SIMON HAS A B.A. IN ENGLISH LITERATURE FROM CARLETON COLLEGE and an M.A. in English literature from the University of Chicago. She began her publishing career in Boston, in the children's book division of Little, Brown and Company. She also spent 6 years as an editor at *Cricket* magazine before becoming a full-time author. Simon has written more than 40 books for kids, and numerous magazine stories and articles. In addition to writing and freelance editing, she is also a contributing editor for *Click* magazine. Simon lives in Madison, Wisconsin, with her husband Tom, their daughters, Ariel and Hana, Sam the dog, and Lily and Luna the cats.